# 50 BARMIEST BIBLE STORIES

# 50 BARMIEST BIBLE STORIES

Andy Robb

**CWR**

# INTRO

There are some things that are really difficult to do, such as eating jelly with a pair of chopsticks, not slurping through the straw when you get to the bottom of a milkshake and keeping a straight face when someone accidentally burps in the middle of quiet reading at school. But for most people, reading the Bible tops the lot of them.

If you've never so much as taken a sneaky peek between the covers of a Bible (and even if you have), it's sometimes really head-scratchingly tricky to know where exactly to begin. For starters, the Bible isn't one big book, it's lots of smaller books (sixty-six actually) that are all crammed together like a mini-library. The books have all got fancy names, such as Genesis (which is right at the very beginning), Job (pronounced JOBE), Psalms (pronounced SARMS), Mark (which you'll be relieved to know is

actually pronounced MARK), Habakkuk (which should get you a pretty good score in a game of Scrabble) and Revelation (which is right at the very end).

Just to make it even more complicated, some of the books have got more than one section (like a sort of Part One and Part Two), and each Bible book doesn't just have chapters like normal books do, they have verses as well (like you get in poems).

So, if you wanted to have a read of chapter 20 and verse 7 of the second book of Kings (cos there are two of them), you may find it written like this …

## 2 Kings 20:7

… which, to me, looks more like a maths equation than anything to do with the Bible – but that's the way it is.

If you're itching to know what that Bible reference I just used is all about and also to find out how some perfectly good figs were (in my opinion) wasted, then you're going to need to get your hands on a copy of a Bible to

check it out. In fact, you'll need
a Bible to get the most out of this
book, so beg, borrow or buy
yourself one as soon as you can.

As it's not always easy to
decide which bit of the Bible to read first and
in what order you should read it, we've gone and done all
the hard work for you. Aren't we kind? In this book are fifty
hand-picked Bible stories which are retold in a zappy style
and with a colourful cartoon to stop you getting bored. At
the end of each story you'll get the chance to find out what
happens next (we don't tell you, you've got to do that for
yourself – aren't we spoilsports?), and that's when you get to
use your Bible. Using the info that we give you about where
to find the story in the Bible, you'll need to look it up and
then see how the story finishes.

That's about it.

Happy reading
and off you go!

# 1
# THE NAME GAME

Some people have the weirdest names, don't they? I'll bet you can think of someone you know who's called something unusual. Choosing a name for a child is always a tricky one for parents because the kid has got to live with it for the rest of their life. So, imagine having to give a name to every living creature on the face of the earth. I don't mean calling them things like Walter or Winifred; I mean names like wombat, wolf and whale.

Let me introduce you to the chap who actually had that job. His name was Adam and, if you didn't know it already, he was the world's first fella.

By the time that God made Adam, every type of animal you could ever think of had been created.

The earth was positively teeming with creatures; on the ground; in the air and under the sea. So why had God given Adam this ginormous job? I'll tell you. God had made the earth (and everything in it) as the home for the pinnacle of His creation: human beings. Although it might sound a bit barmy to some people, God's plan was to hand the whole kit and caboodle (that means everything) over to us so that we could take care of His wonderful handiwork.

Giving all the animals a name was part of this. It's like God was saying, 'Right Adam, you're running this show now. Call them whatever you want.' The Bible doesn't give us a clue how long it took the world's first man to give all the animals a name but I guess it would have taken quite some time. To be honest nobody really knows how many different creatures there are on the earth although plenty of people have tried to work it out. The chances are it's into many millions which makes me think that Adam must have been a pretty smart guy – not only to have come up with all the names but to have remembered them as well!

# BRICK BOTHER

**M**oses (and his big brother, Aaron) were heading for a rendezvous with Egypt's Pharaoh. God had sent the pair of them to tell Egypt's powerful ruler to let his Israelite slaves go free. First off, God wanted them to be allowed to down tools and take a three-day trip out into the desert to make sacrifices to Him. I suppose a mini-break would have been nice for them. It can't have been much fun making bricks out of straw for your Egyptian slave masters day in, day out – just so that they can build bigger and bigger cities. (For your information, straw was used to strengthen the clay bricks that they built with.)

But things didn't quite go as Moses and Aaron planned. Pharaoh thought it was just a cunning ruse to get his whopping great Israelite labour force out of doing their work. Besides, he had no idea who their God was anyway so why on earth should he take a blind bit of notice of their barmy request? In fact it made him so mad he told his slave drivers to make the Israelites find their own straw from now on, but with no slacking. They still had to deliver the same number of bricks but now it was heaps more difficult. While the Israelites worked their fingers to the bone, desperately trying to fulfil their quotas, their slave drivers just accused them of being lazy.

As things got to breaking point the Israelite overseers were at their wits' end. No way could they make the same number of bricks as they'd had to previously at the same time as having to scavenge for their own supply of straw and they told Pharaoh so. He was having none of it. As far as he was concerned it was just a bunch of excuses. On their way out of their meet-up with Pharaoh the overseers bumped into Moses and Aaron and gave them a piece of their mind. If they hadn't interfered then none of this would ever have happened.

That's not how God saw it. He was just giving Pharaoh the chance to do the decent thing. Now things were going to hot up.

To find out how, read Bible book Exodus, chapter 7 and verses 19 to 21.

# SILLY SIHON

I n this Bible story we catch up with the Israelites as they are aimlessly roaming around in the desert. By now they should have been in the land of Canaan which God had given them to settle down in but they'd foolishly chosen not to enter it for fear of the inhabitants. God wasn't particularly happy about their bad decision and made it clear that they'd now have to wait until all the disobedient cowards had died before they got a second chance.

Wandering in the wilderness is not much fun when you've only got tents to live in and can't grow your own food to eat. Fortunately for the Israelites, God had kindly provided them with food but not everyone was quite so obliging. As they roamed from place to place the Israelites passed through lands ruled by various tribes and kings. Chances are that the inhabitants of these lands weren't too happy to have the vast Israelite nation on their doorstep and sometimes they let 'em know it. King Arad (a Canaanite king) had already attacked them along the way, although the Israelites got their own back.

Now the Israelites found themselves sandwiched between the land of the Amorites and the land of the Moabites. If they could just pass through without any fuss, that would be great.

Out of courtesy the Israelites sent messengers to King Sihon

(the Amorite king) to ask if this was okay with him. Their plan was to travel on what was called 'the King's Highway' and they promised not to help themselves to any of the Amorites' crops or water en route. Seemed like a fair request.

Silly Sihon didn't think so. Why do I call him silly? Well, if he knew anything about the Israelites he'd know that God was with them. This meant that if anyone attacked God's special nation then God would defend them. As I mentioned, King Arad had already discovered this to his cost and now King Sihon was about to make the same barmy botch-up as well.

Sure enough Sihon mustered his troops and launched all-out war against the Israelites. Want to know the gory details of what happened? Of course you do!

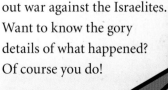

Take a look in Bible book Numbers, chapter 21 and verses 34 and 35.

# NO BRAINER

The barmy Bible story we're going to look at now is all about how God gave the Israelites (His special nation) a simple choice to make. This wasn't something trivial like 'Shall I have custard with my salad?' or 'Do I wear one sock today or two?' – the choice that the Israelites had to make was a matter of life and death.

Here's the deal. As far as God is concerned there's a right way to live and there's a wrong way to live. Do things God's way and everything will be hunky-dory (fine). Do things any old way you want and it'll be bad news. Just like there are rules that you need to obey when crossing the road (to keep you safe), so there are rules that God has made to make sure that things go well for us.

God's rules were all about obeying Him. The reason obeying God was so important is that at the beginning of time the world's first man and woman (Adam and Eve) disobeyed God and, as a result, lost His blessing on their lives. God's blessing is simply God looking after us and providing us with everything we need.

God is a good God and He'd hand-picked the Israelites to show the rest of the world what a loving God He is. Once He'd got them back on board the way would be open for everyone else.

Here's a flavour of some of the blessings that were on offer for obeying God: Their women would have no problems having kids and their animals would multiply. At harvest time their barns would be stacked to the rafters. They'd have God's protection from enemy attack. Whatever they set their hands to would be successful. In fact, God promised that every area of their lives would be blessed. Wherever they went and whatever they did, it would go well for them. Sounds too good to be true but it was there for the taking.

The flip side of this was that if they chose to do their own thing and ignore God the Israelites wouldn't just miss out on all these goodies; the complete opposite would happen and everything would go belly up. Put it like that and they'd have been barmy not to obey God. And, just in case they were barmy enough to think about not doing things God's way, He had some handy advice for them.

HMM!
A TRICKY
DECISION,
GOD!

Check it out in Bible book Deuteronomy, chapter 30 and verses 19 and 20.

# 5
# BARMY ARMY

Joshua and the Israelites were on the warpath. Bit by bit they were advancing through the land of Canaan conquering towns and cities as they went. God had given them the land to settle in but first off they needed to rid the place of its wicked inhabitants. With Jericho already done and dusted Joshua and his troops were ready for their next conquest. With God on their side they were invincible!

Joshua sent spies to check out the city of Ai. When the spies returned it was with good news. They told Joshua that it was going to be easy peasy (or words to that effect). Ai wasn't that big and its people would be no match for their army. In fact, don't bother sending all their fighting men. Three thousand should do it, no probs. So off to war the Israelites went.

But unfortunately for Joshua, things didn't quite go to plan. As the Israelites launched their attack on the city they were ambushed by the army of Ai and sent scurrying with their tails between their legs. The Bible says that thirty-six Israelites were killed in the skirmish and the rest of them escaped by the skin of their teeth. What a disaster! Joshua was mortified and fell face down before God wanting to know what was going on. God told Joshua to get to his feet. The reason for their defeat was because one of them had disobeyed God, so

He'd lifted His hand of protection from them all.

When the Israelites had attacked Jericho, God had specifically said not to take anything for themselves, such as gold, silver, valuables, that sort of thing. But some barmy person had ignored God's warning and now they were all suffering the consequences.

Right, time to find the culprit! Next day Joshua had the world's biggest identity parade to find out who was to blame. Tribe by tribe, clan by clan and family by family they lined up before Joshua until he was left with a guy called Achan. Achan finally came clean and admitted that he'd given in to temptation and nicked a load of booty which he'd hidden under his tent.

Want to find out what happened to Achan? Rush to Bible book Joshua, chapter 7 and read verses 22 to 26.

# 6
# WOEFUL WEAPONS

If you take a look through the Old Testament bit of the Bible you'll soon discover that of all the enemies Israel had, the Philistines seemed to niggle them the most. Maybe this was because they were next door neighbours but, whatever the reason, the bottom line is that the two of them just didn't get on one little bit and they were forever looking for ways to get at each other.

Israel's first ever king was a chap named Saul and he wasted no time in stirring things up between the Israelites and the pesky Philistines. Actually it was Saul's son Jonathan who got things started by bravely attacking a Philistine outpost. Okay, so Saul claimed the credit but either way it was sure to tick off the Philistines. Just what Israel's new king was hoping for and he told everyone so.

The Philistines retaliated by sending a mahoosive army designed to teach the Israelites a lesson they'd never forget. The Bible handily tells us that there were 3,000 chariots, 6,000 charioteers, and soldiers as numerous as the sand on the seashore. Just one itty bitty problem. The Bible also helpfully tells us the size of Saul's army. A not-quite-so-mahoosive 3,000. Gulp!

But that's not the end of it. After seeing the size of their enemy Saul's men panicked and began to desert him in their

droves until he was down to just a measly 600 men. As if that wasn't enough, Israel didn't have one single blacksmith in the land. The Philistines had banned the Israelites from having them. Er, what's that got to do with it you ask?

Without blacksmiths to sharpen their swords Saul's army were at a disadvantage because they'd only have blunt weapons to fight with. That didn't really matter because the Israelites also weren't allowed to have weapons (with the odd exception) anyway. The only thing they did have (with which to fight their enemy) were farm tools such as axes and sickles. How barmy was that? To add insult to injury, the Philistines cheekily charged for sharpening them.

Want to take a peek at what the Israelite army looked like on the day of the battle? Go to Bible book 1 Samuel, chapter 13 and verse 22.

# FOR THE CHOP

**W**e drop in on this barmy Bible story soon after a guy called Joshua had died. He'd been the leader of the Israelite nation for many years after taking over from Moses. Joshua had led them to victory after victory as they sought to conquer the land of Canaan. Well, most of it that is. There were some pockets of the country that still remained in enemy control which made things a tad difficult for the Israelites.

I suppose that it was like living in your own house but having squatters in some of the rooms. Not much fun! Although it was your home you could never quite relax. That's why the Israelites felt rather uneasy. They couldn't fully settle down and get on with the day-to-day business of life all the while their enemies were lurking just a short distance away.

There was only one thing for it. They had to drive these last remaining interlopers out of the land for good.

With their leader, Joshua, dead and buried it was now up to the tribal leaders to run the show. The tribe of Judah had a word with the tribe of Simeon and persuaded them to join forces to drive the Canaanites and the Perizzites out of their land once and for all.

The Bible says that God was on their side and the Canaanites and the Perizzites took a right old hammering. At a place called Bezek the Israelites slaughtered 10,000 of their enemy. They now had them on the back foot and pursued their foe without mercy. Adoni Bezek (the Canaanite king) fled for his life but the Israelites were too quick for him and he was eventually caught.

What happened next is a bit gruesome I have to say and if you are a little bit squeamish, then perhaps it's best that you just skip to the next story in this book.

Here goes. To make 100 per cent certain that King Adoni Bezek never again held a sword and to stop him marching into war ever again, the Israelites cut off both his thumbs and both his big toes. Yuck! Was this way of treating captured kings a surprise to Adoni Bezek?

Find out in Bible book Judges, chapter 1 and verse 7.

# PRIESTS DECEASED

erving in God's tabernacle (the Israelites' tent for worshipping God) was a super-serious business and most definitely not one you took lightly. In this Bible story we catch up with a priest called Eli who was the tabernacle's main man at that time. Eli had a couple of wayward sons (Hophni and Phineas) who worked for the family business and were also priests. To all intents and purposes it seems like Eli was a bit of a walkover when it came to parenting and his two boys just about got away with murder (not literally of course).

God was well-peeved with the casual attitude of Hophni and Phineas. They seemed to care little or nothing for God and an awful lot for how they could use their important job to please themselves. Eli's sons were absolute scoundrels.

One of the best bits of being a priest was looking after the golden ark box which was kept in the tabernacle. The box represented God being with the Israelites so it needed protecting day and night. After suffering a nasty defeat against the Philistine army the Israelites decided to go and fetch the ark and take it with them into battle. Surely with the ark alongside them victory was guaranteed. Not so fast. The ark box wasn't just some sort of lucky charm. It didn't work like that. First off there

was still the matter of Hophni and Phineas' misdemeanours. As far as God was concerned their time was up.

As soon as the Philistines found out that God's ark was in the Israelite camp they were all for giving up. But while the victory shouts of the Israelites thundered over the battlefield the Philistines got a grip on themselves and decided that they were not going to go quietly. The battle was vicious but the Philistines won the day.

Hophni and Phineas did not escape and were both killed. Not only that, but the ark was captured by the Philistines. Eli had been watching the battle from a distance and, when news reached him of what had happened, he fell backwards off his chair, broke his neck and died. The Bible says that he was old (ninety-eight to be precise) and heavy. What a barmy way to go! It doesn't end there though.

Head for Bible book 1 Samuel, chapter 4 and read verses 19 to 22.

# 'AM I BOVVERED?'

ho's the barmiest Christian in the New Testament part of the Bible? Without a shadow of a doubt it has to be a guy called Paul. Paul wasn't barmy in a mad sort of way but he didn't seem to mind putting himself in the way of danger if it meant he had the chance to tell people about Jesus. Paul was now heading for Jerusalem (Israel's capital city) after to-ing and fro-ing around the Mediterranean region doing great things for God. Paul was a human dynamo and everywhere he went he seemed to stir up trouble from people who didn't want anything to do with Jesus. Paul didn't mind this one little bit. So long as people were talking about Jesus that was all that mattered.

After travelling over land and sea Paul was on the final leg of his trip and was now heading down the coast towards Jerusalem. His friends sensed that there was trouble lurking around the corner and they urged Paul to think twice about continuing his journey. Paul was having none of it. He wasn't going to be put off by a spot of bother.

Jerusalem was getting nearer by the day and with only about forty to fifty miles left to go Paul took a break for a few days at a place called Caesarea. Just for your info the Bible tells us that he stayed with a fella called Philip the evangelist

and his four daughters. (Thought you'd like to know that.)
After a few days Paul had an unexpected visitor. A prophet
called Agabus turned up from Judea with a personal message
from God to Paul. How nice! Was it to give Paul a pat on the
back and tell him 'well done'? 'Fraid not. Agabus took Paul's
belt and used it to tie Paul's hands and feet. What sort of
message was this? All was about to be revealed. The prophet
told Paul that God was giving him a heads-up that when he
reached Jerusalem the Jews were going to tie him up like this
and hand him over to the Gentiles (people who weren't Jews).

His friends pleaded with
him not to go but no
amount of weeping and
wailing was going to
change Paul's mind.

Did what Agabus said
actually happen?
All is revealed in Bible book
Acts, chapter 21 and verses
27 to 33.

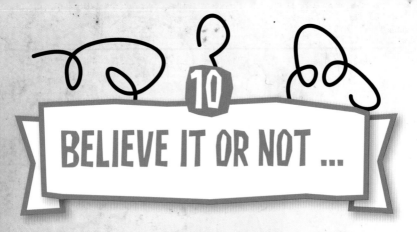

# BELIEVE IT OR NOT ...

The Bible is not only full of loads and loads of brilliant stuff about God; it's also got heaps of fascinating facts.

For instance, did you know that dinosaur-like creatures are mentioned in the book of Job (check out Bible book Job, chapter 40 and verses 15 to 24) or that you can find out from the Bible how long the world's oldest man lived for (check out Bible book Genesis, chapter 5 and verse 27)?

But did you also know the Bible had adverts in it? Yep, I'm serious. Before Jesus came to earth (from heaven) God gave the world a heads-up that He was on the way. The Bible calls these adverts prophecies. They told people where Jesus was going to be born (check out Bible book Micah, chapter 5 and verse 2) and what He was going to do (check out Bible book Isaiah, chapter 35 and verses 5 and 6). Wow!

And the Bible has also got funny stuff in it if you fancy a bit of a giggle.

There's a story about Israel's King Saul using a cave as a loo (check out Bible book 1 Samuel, chapter 24 and verses 1 to 3) and another one about when Jesus paid for His taxes in the funniest of ways (check out Bible book Matthew, chapter 17 and verses 24 to 27).

Something else that you may not have realised is that football gets a mention in the Bible too (well sort of). In Bible book Acts, chapter 13 and from verses 1 to 3 it says that the church in Antioch packed off a couple of guys called Paul and Barnabas to go and do a special job for God. What's that got to do with football? Well, in my Bible the heading for this story is 'Barnabas and Saul Sent Off'! In a moment of barminess it can look like they got red cards for fouling someone in a football match.

And finally, how about this for a spot of yet more barminess? In the Old Testament part of the Bible it mentions a fella called King Og (of Bashan). This mahoosive monarch was so tall that he slept in a four metre bed. Now that's what you call having a long lie in!

Does God ever have a chuckle? Find out in Bible book Psalms, chapter 2 and verse 4.

# 11
# BARMY BABBLERS?

Once upon a time people all spoke the same language. What that language was nobody knows but all that changed when the early inhabitants of the world started to get a bit too big for their boots. These Smart Alecs figured that if they joined forces they'd be clever enough and powerful enough to do anything they wanted (without the need for God). God had given them strict instructions to populate the earth but their plan was to settle down in one place. God soon put a stop to that nonsense by confusing their language so that they couldn't understand a word each other was saying. How frustrating! There was little choice but to move away and find somewhere else to live and to settle with people who spoke the same language as them.

The barmy Bible story we're going to look at occurred thousands of years later and in the city of Jerusalem. Most of its inhabitants spoke Aramaic and Greek but the busy city was often full of visitors from other lands as well who'd rocked up for one or other of Jerusalem's religious festivals. On this occasion it was the Jewish festival of Pentecost and the place was positively heaving with people from far and wide.

Meanwhile, in an upstairs room somewhere in the city, some followers of Jesus were having a bit of a get-together.

They'd been told by Jesus (before He'd gone back to heaven) to wait for the gift of the Holy Spirit. The Holy Spirit would empower them to do the same things Jesus had been doing. In fact, Jesus had called the Holy Spirit, the Helper, because He knew that they would need help. The Holy Spirit isn't just a power, He is a Person.

Sure enough the Holy Spirit did come just like Jesus had said. The Holy Spirit looked like tongues of fire from heaven and sounded like the whooshing of the wind. But there was more to come. Filled up with God's power everyone started speaking in languages that they'd never spoken before. As they spilled out into the milling crowd people thought that they were completely barmy. Did the onlookers have the foggiest idea what these power-packed followers of Jesus were on about or was it just a load of mumbo jumbo?

Find out in Bible book Acts, chapter 2 and verses 5 to 11.

# YOU BIG BABY

Jesus was a bit of a headache for the Jewish religious leaders of His day. The crowds absolutely loved Jesus because of the way He taught them about God with such authority (He was God's Son after all) and because of the way He healed them of their sicknesses. The religious leaders on the other hand had rather lost the plot. They'd reduced everything down to a list of rules and regulations that you had to keep to stay in God's good books. But God, for His part, wanted people to get to know Him and then from that live lives that pleased Him, without doing everything out of a sense of duty.

It has to be said that not all of the religious leaders were against Jesus. A guy called Nicodemus (who was a top bod in religious circles) was a bit more open-minded about God's Son. That said, there was no way that Nicodemus wanted anybody to know this, so, under cover of darkness, he had a top secret meet-up with Jesus. It was pretty obvious to Nicodemus that Jesus wouldn't have been able to do any of the healings and miracles if God wasn't with Him. In fact the Bible tells us that Nicodemus lets on that he wasn't the only one who thought like this. It was clear to him (and others) that Jesus had been sent by God but they couldn't quite figure out how He fitted into their religious way of doing things. Jesus had an answer for this conundrum.

He told Nicodemus what sounded like the barmiest thing the bemused religious leader had ever heard. Jesus said that to know God and to understand Him, you had to be born again. What? Did he hear Jesus right? There was no way a man like him was ever going to get back inside his mum's tum. What Jesus meant was that getting to know God is like having a new start in life. Jesus was soon going to die to take the punishment for all the bad things in our lives. When we accept His sacrifice for us, His Holy Spirit makes us new inside and that's what it means to be born again. So, who gets the chance to be born again?

# 13

# TEMPLE TWOSOME

This Bible story is based around Jerusalem's Temple shortly after Jesus had been born. Because Jesus was Jewish, His mum and dad (Mary and Joseph) had to perform certain religious rituals for their new-born baby. One of these involved paying a visit to the Temple to present the child to God. Fortunately for them they only lived a few miles away in Bethlehem so it wasn't a long trip.

In keeping with Jewish law, Mary and Joseph also had to sacrifice a pair of doves or pigeons to God. During the course of this Temple trip something rather odd happened. A godly guy called Simeon had been waiting years for the day when Israel's Messiah (someone sent by God to save them) would show up, and now the day had finally arrived. God's Holy Spirit led Simeon to the Temple courts ready for his meet-up with the Messiah. When Simeon clapped eyes on Jesus he knew that He was the One he'd been waiting for. He strode up to Jesus' mum and dad, took hold of Jesus and then began to spout a load of stuff that God had given him to say. It was all to do with who Jesus was, what He would become and how He would change the world.

I'll bet Mary and Joseph were a little bit gobsmacked. Well, if they were, they didn't have long to think about it. Before

the pair of them had time to catch breath, a second visitor arrived. Her name was Anna and the Bible tells us that she was eighty-four years old. Anna was a prophetess (which is just a female prophet) and had lived for most of her life in and around the Temple spending her time fasting, praying and worshipping. Anna immediately knew that Jesus was the Saviour Israel had been waiting for and blabbed about it to anyone who would listen. Did Mary and Joseph stay in Jerusalem to bask in the glory of having such a special Son?

Look in Bible book Luke, chapter 2 and verses 39 to 40 to see.

Y ou might have heard of the star of this barmy Bible story, his name was Isaac. Isaac's dad was one hundred years old when he was born (and his mum, Sarah, was ninety). Isaac had taken over from his dad as leader of the Israelite nation. As we drop in on this story a nasty famine has hit the land of Canaan where Isaac lived. There was nothing for it but to up sticks and find someone who could supply them with food and water. Off they trundled to Gerar where Abimelech (the Philistine king) hung out. Yep, he was up for it! The Israelites could stay until things got better. How kind was that? Because the Israelites were God's special nation God kept an eye on them even when they were in another land. Everything the Israelites did succeeded because God was blessing them. When they planted crops they reaped a whopper of a harvest. And they had so many flocks and herds that the Philistines became green with envy.

It was one thing sharing their land with the Israelites because of the famine but another thing seeing God's people get richer than them. They weren't going to put up with that. So the barmy Philistines decided to fill up the Israelites' wells. Spoilsports!

It wasn't only Abimelech's subjects who were getting a bit jittery about the Israelites' rapid expansion. He was as well. Enough was

enough. King Abimelech told Isaac that they were becoming a threat to the Philistines and that it was time to move on. Which is precisely what the Israelites did. They settled in the Valley of Gerar and re-opened the wells that had been blocked up.

Just to prove to the Philistines that God loved to bless His special nation they dug a new well and discovered a new supply of fresh water. But, once again the Philistines were jealous and said that the water was theirs. So the Israelites dug another well and, surprise, surprise, the Philistines kicked up another fuss. Maybe if they just trusted God He'd look after them too.

One more time the Israelites went digging for fresh water and once again they found it.

Want to discover if the Philistines got their hands on this well, as well (pardon the pun)?

Go to Bible book Genesis, chapter 26 and verse 22 to find out.

# 15
# RIOTOUS RULES

In the Old Testament bit of the Bible there are loads and loads of laws that God expected the Israelite nation to keep. To be frank, some of them can seem a little bit barmy if you don't understand why God made them. Let me explain.

God had created Israel to remind the world what He was like and that He was alive and kicking. Not only that, but God was going to use Israel as the base for His Son, Jesus, when He eventually visited earth. Because God is 100 per cent good it was really important that the Israelites reflected this. So, their job was to show the rest of the world exactly what God is like.

To cut them some slack God knew that they wouldn't always make the grade but He wanted them at least to give it their best shot. Which is why God gave the Israelites the laws that I was talking about. Some of them were to keep the Israelites on the right track with God and some were to protect them. Isn't God kind?

I'll bet you're now wondering what some of those laws were, aren't you? Well listen up and I'll tell you.

For starters there were laws about some of the things that they weren't allowed to eat such as weasels, rats, geckos, any kind of great lizard, the monitor lizard, the wall lizard, the skink and the chameleon.

Who fancies a lizard burger and fries or how about a weasel casserole? Call me barmy but I don't think I'd need to be told not to have them on the menu. I reckon I'd pass on the lot of 'em.

Next up, how about these no-nos?

Do not cut the hair at the sides of your head or clip off the edges of your beard.

Do not cut your bodies for the dead or put tattoo marks on yourselves.

Do not go to mediums or wizards.

Fancy taking a look at some more of these laws?

# CRAZY KING

**N**asty Nahash (king of Ammon) had his sights set on conquering the town of Jabesh Gilead. Between you and me, the inhabitants of the place weren't too keen on the idea. In those days an enemy attack usually meant getting wiped out and that really didn't sound like much fun to the Jabesh Gileadites (I just made that name up – I haven't a clue what you would call people who lived there). As a last resort they tried to make a peace treaty with King Nahash but he wasn't too struck on the idea. To be fair, he did offer to meet them half way. His helpful suggestion was how about if he gouged everyone's right eye out first and then he'd think about a treaty? How did that sound? Hmm, not too appealing actually but thanks for asking.

Realising that they were on the back foot, the leaders of Jabesh Gilead had a brainwave. Supposing the cruel king (not that they called him that to his face) gave them seven days' breathing space? In the meantime they'd send out messengers into all Israel to see if anyone would come to their rescue. If I'd been Nahash I would have said no way. Why make things harder for yourself!

Who knows if Nahash had sent his brains to the cleaners on that particular day or whether he just wasn't thinking

straight but of all the barmy things, he said yes to their brazen request. Hardly the smartest move on his part was it?

When word of the imminent attack of Jabesh Gilead reached the ears of a chap called Saul he was livid. Grrr!

God's Spirit came on him in power and the Bible says he chopped up a couple of oxen. Saul sent them by special delivery to the four corners of Israel with a warning that anyone who didn't join him to fight King Nahash would suffer the same fate as the unfortunate oxen.

No surprise then that a fearsome fighting force of 330,000 mustered to take out the Ammonites.

Did Nahash live to regret giving the people of Jabesh Gilead a seven-day window of opportunity?

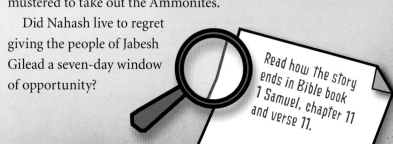

Read how the story ends in Bible book 1 Samuel, chapter 11 and verse 11.

# GREEDY GEHAZI

The Bible bit that we're going to look at now is the second part of a well-known Bible story. It features a guy called Namaan who was the commander of the king of Aram's army.

Namaan had been suffering with a horrid skin disease called leprosy and had travelled to see the prophet Elisha to see if he could make him better. Elisha couldn't but God's power could. Elisha had told Namaan to take a dip in the river Jordan seven times and he'd be healed. Job done! After a bit of mumbling and grumbling about Elisha's odd way of doing things Namaan did as he was told and the leprosy disappeared.

Namaan was so pleased to be well again that he wanted to give Elisha a thank you present. Nope. Elisha wouldn't think of it. As far as the prophet was concerned it was God who performed the miracle and God who deserved the credit. Fair enough.

Namaan promised that from then on he would worship only Elisha's God and not the idols his nation worshipped.

When Namaan had said his goodbyes, Elisha's servant, Gehazi, had a thing or two to say to his master. He was none-too-pleased that the army commander had got off scot-free without it costing him a penny. A man in his position would be loaded and Gehazi thought that Elisha had missed a trick by not asking for some goodies in return for his miracle. Gehazi sneaked off and raced after Namaan.

When Namaan saw Gehazi approaching he got down from his chariot to find out what was up. Gehazi spun him a yarn that a couple of impoverished prophets had suddenly showed up and needed cash and clothes. The grateful commander believed the lie, hook, line and sinker, stumped up what Gehazi was asking for and then they went their separate ways.

The barmy servant should have known better than to go behind his master's back. Elisha had a bit of a reputation for God telling him what people were up to and Gehazi was no exception. Elisha knew full well what greedy Gehazi had been up to and it was now pay-back time.

WHAT MAKES YOU THINK I'M GREEDY?

Discover what this meant in Bible book 2 Kings, chapter 5 and verses 26 and 27.

# EWE ROTTER

The Bible tells us that King David of Israel was a man after God's own heart. That means he cared for the things that God cared about and that he made God No. 1 in his life.

David was Israel's second ever king (Saul had been the first) and he was a big hit with just about everyone. He'd made a name for himself by killing the Philistine giant, Goliath, with a single stone to his head and then lopping the giant's head off. After that David led the Israelites to victory over their arch enemy, the Philistines.

Not bad for a shepherd boy from Bethlehem!

Soon after he became Israel's king, David made an almighty boo-boo by falling head over heels in love with Bathsheba (the wife of a guy called Uriah). The long and the short of it is that, while Uriah was away fighting with the Israelite army, David seduced Bathsheba. When Bathsheba fell pregnant with the king's baby, David panicked and tried to cover his tracks but he failed miserably. If David didn't do something soon Uriah would find out that he'd got up to some hanky panky with his wife. Barmy as it may seem, as a last resort David gave the order for poor unsuspecting Uriah to be sent to the front lines of battle where he was almost guaranteed to be killed outright. And sure enough, that's

what happened. Bathsheba's hubbie copped it in the heat of
battle and David was now free to marry the new love of his
life. It looked like the king had got away with it this time. Or
at least that's what David thought.

Then, one day, out of the blue, Nathan the prophet turned
up with a story to tell.

The story was about two men who lived in the same town.
One of them was stinking rich and the other had barely
enough to scrape by. While the rich man had more sheep and
cattle than he knew what to do with, the poor man had one
solitary ewe lamb which was like part of his family.

One day a visitor dropped by at the rich man's house
but instead of killing one of his own sheep for a meal,
he went and nabbed the
poor man's ewe lamb and
killed it instead. How
mean was that?

Find out why Nathan
told this story by
heading for Bible book
2 Samuel, chapter 12
and verses 5 to 10.

**N**ebuchadnezzar (king of Babylon) was a bit perplexed. He'd had a dream that had left him feeling a little uneasy. Unlike some dreams that seem to evaporate as soon as you try to remember them, this vivid dream would not go away. The king was disturbed and wanted to know what it meant. He summoned his magicians and astrologers to see if they could interpret it but they were a fat lot of use. They hadn't the foggiest idea what the dream was about. So a chap called Daniel was sent for. Daniel was a Jew who had been captured and taken to live in Babylon's royal household and trained in its ways. Daniel already had a bit of reputation for interpreting Nebuchadnezzar's dreams so hopes were high. (For the record, Daniel had made clear that if it hadn't been for God giving him this ability he wouldn't be able to do it.)

Anyway, King Nebuchadnezzar's dream went something like this. In it he'd seen a towering tree that touched the sky. Its branches stretched far and wide and its leafy limbs were hung with fruit and filled with the birds of the air. So far, so good.

Then an angel from God gave the command for the tree to be chopped down and just to leave a stump.

No point in beating about the bush. Daniel told the king

straight. The tree represented Nebuchadnezzar and the great power that he had. Unfortunately he had misused it and now God was going to call time on his reign and reduce him to almost nothing (like the tree stump). King Nebuchadnezzar's fall would be so great and so swift (like a felled tree) that he would be driven barmy and spend seven years living in the countryside like a wild animal.

The king completely ignored Daniel's advice to turn from his wicked ways. One year later, as Nebuchadnezzar was strutting on the roof of his palace and telling himself how great he was, the dream turned into the nightmare he'd predicted. He was driven away and lived like a wild animal just like Daniel had said.

I DON'T FEEL SO GREAT NOW!

Want to see how the story ends? Turn to Bible book Daniel, chapter 4 and verses 34 to 37.

# DIVINE DUNKER

I f you go to see a TV show being recorded there's often a warm-up person who comes on before it to get the audience in a good mood. When it comes to the Bible, John the Baptist was Jesus' warm-up man. Not that he set out to put people in a good mood, but get them ready he most certainly did. John was a close relative of Jesus and he had been born just a few months ahead of Him. The star of this barmy Bible story had been lined up from the word go to announce to the world that Jesus was on His way. That was going to be his life's work and John took his job seriously.

We catch up with John in the Judean desert wearing a rather uncomfortable camel-hair tunic held together by a natty belt around his waist. As if that wasn't barmy enough you should hear about his diet. Locusts and wild honey! They say that a spoonful of sugar helps the medicine go down but I reckon you'd need an awful lot of honey to take away the taste of a locust. Yuckky yoo!

Although he was living out in the back of beyond John had attracted quite a lot of interest because of what he had to say. His message was that people needed to repent (that means to turn around). Turn around from what? From leading lives that make do without God, that's what!

John was giving people the chance to turn from their wicked ways by being baptised (that's how he got his nickname of 'Baptist') in the nearby River Jordan. Being baptised simply means getting dunked completely in water to represent all the grot in your life being washed away by God.

One day, who should show up but Jesus Himself? (Just for your info, Jesus is God's Son.) Jesus was now around thirty years old and for all of that time He hadn't stepped over the line even once. The Bible says that there was no sin (stuff we do wrong) to be found in Jesus whatsoever. Wow! But here's the amazing thing. Jesus still wanted to be baptised by John.

It has to be said that John couldn't believe it either. Surely not! This was barmy. Jesus should be baptising him.

To discover who baptised who, check out Bible book Matthew, chapter 3 and verses 13 to 17.

There was probably only one person who narked the Jewish religious leaders more than Jesus and it was a fella called Paul. Paul was actually a follower of Jesus and he'd made it his business to tell the world that Jesus was God's Son who'd come to earth to give us all a second chance with God. The reason these religious leaders didn't take too kindly to Paul is because they didn't believe that Jesus was the Messiah (a special person sent by God) that the Jews had been waiting for.

Paul had been arrested by the Romans for disrupting the peace after a crowd of angry Jews had nearly lynched him. Next up he was brought before the Jewish Sanhedrin (a meeting of the Jewish big shots) to explain himself. In no time at all this also turned nasty and once again Paul had to be rescued by the Romans (they'd since found out he was actually a Roman citizen) before he was torn to shreds.

While Paul was safely under lock and key in a Roman fort, word reached him that a plot had been hatched by a group of angry Jews to kill him. The plan was to get Paul out from the protection of the Romans back to the Sanhedrin court – under the pretence of needing to ask him some more questions – and then to ambush him along the way. But Paul got his nephew to tell the Romans just what monkey business the Jews were planning, and Lysias (the Roman commander) lost no time in doing something to stop it. At dead of night, he rallied 200 of his officers, 70 cavalry and 200 armed soldiers to escort Paul to Caesarea and into the safekeeping of its governor, Felix.

Surprise surprise, five days later the Jewish high priest turned up with some elders and a lawyer (named Tertullus) in tow. They tried to smooth-talk Governor Felix into handing Paul over to them but Felix wasn't stupid. He knew what their game was.

What happened next? Did Paul get released?

I DIDN'T REALISE I WAS SO POPULAR!

WANTED

PAUL

Find out by reading Bible book Acts, chapter 24 and verses 22 to 27.

# GETTING THE HUMP

**W**herever Jesus went, often as not He would attract a large crowd of people champing at the bit to hear what He had to say and hanging on to His every word. Sometimes Jesus used stories (called parables) to explain things about God and sometimes He would simply use His surroundings to help get the message across. For instance, one time when Jesus was teaching people about trusting God and not worrying, He pointed to some lilies growing nearby and said that there was an important lesson we could learn from them and it was this – they don't get stressed and anxious about things but still, they blossom into beautiful flowers.

And then Jesus drew their attention to some birds flying above and said that likewise they don't fret about where their next meal is coming from – but God takes care of them as well.

As far as God is concerned we are heaps more valuable than both the birds and the flowers so quit worrying.

But the Bible bit we're heading for now has caused a lot of head scratching over the years trying to work out what exactly Jesus meant.

A wealthy young man approached Jesus and flung himself at His feet. He had a big question for Jesus and he was expecting a big answer. The chap wanted to know how he could guarantee

himself a place in heaven when he died. Good question! It wasn't as if the young man had lived a reckless life and been a bad boy. He assured Jesus that he'd done his level best to keep all of God's commandments since childhood. No problem there then.

Right, so how about he go and sell everything he owned and give the proceeds to the poor? That should do it. The guy was mortified. Anything but that!

Why did Jesus tell him to give away everything he had? Simple. Jesus knew that this guy's wealth was the most important thing in his life. It wasn't that Jesus was against people being rich but He also knew that making God No. 1 in your life was the only way to live.

The visual aid Jesus used to explain what He was saying sounds really barmy.

See what you think it means by looking up Bible book Mark, chapter 10 and verses 24 and 25.

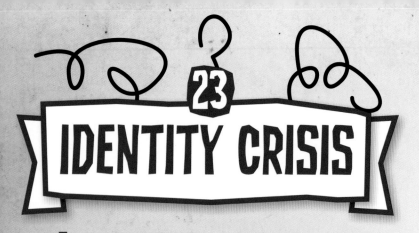

# IDENTITY CRISIS

**J**esus had been brought up in the town of Nazareth where He'd lived with His mum, dad, brothers and sisters. The Bible tells us that Jesus' dad made his living as a carpenter and there's every chance that Jesus joined the family business.

Other than a story about Jesus going to Jerusalem with His family when He was twelve years old the Bible says absolutely zilch about Jesus' upbringing. The chances are that He was brought up like any normal Jewish boy. He would have been taught all about God from the Jewish Scriptures and His dad would have had a big part to play in that. Although Jesus' mum and dad (Mary and Joseph) had been told by God that their boy was going to be a special lad (well actually He was God's Son so that makes Him more than a little special I'd say), we've no idea if they blabbed about this to their family and friends or whether they just kept schtum (said nothing). That said, it's fairly safe to assume that as far as most people were concerned, Jesus was nothing out of the ordinary.

But that was all about to change. Jesus had hit the ripe old age of thirty and this was where the fun began. Jesus was on a mission to patch things up between us and God and, after thirty years of waiting in the wings, it was now time for Him to go centre stage. Having been filled with God's Holy Spirit (which was His power to do the job), Jesus sprung into action.

With a tip-top team of twelve guys to help Him, Jesus went from place to place teaching people about God and healing the sick. It didn't take long for word to get out about this miracle-working man from Nazareth. He was soon making a bit of a name for Himself and wherever Jesus went the crowds gathered.

Next stop for Jesus was His home town. I wonder what they'd make of the carpenter's son now? Time to find out. On the Jewish Sabbath (Saturday) Jesus headed for the synagogue (where the Jews had 'church') and began to teach them what He knew about God. They were gobsmacked. Where did this guy get such wisdom from? And come to think of it, how did He do all those miracles?

Want to find out if the people of Nazareth joined Jesus' fan club?

One of the best ways to bamboozle yourself is to try and work out what things were like before the universe was formed. Okay so you might come to the conclusion that there was nothing but nothingness, but that still leaves the question: what does nothingness actually look like? And come to think of it, what was there before God or has God always existed? And then again who made God? (To which the answer is nobody – God has always been around.) Had enough of being bamboozled? Is your brain ready to explode? Well don't let that happen quite yet because you're going to need it to have a good old ponder over our next barmy Bible bit.

In Bible book Genesis (the very first book in the Bible) it tells us how our universe, the world we live in and everything in it, was created. It tells us that there was once a time when there was absolutely nothing. Then God decided to change all that. Although the place that God lived in (heaven) was full of wonderful beings like angels, He had it in His head to create something altogether different.

What He had in mind was to create beings (human beings) who He could love and who would love Him back. Humans would have their own world in which to live and God had planned it down to the last detail. Now the time had come to make it happen.

The Bible says that God gave the order for things to start appearing and, as if by magic (but actually by the power of God's Holy Spirit), they did. The first thing to show up was planet Earth. It didn't look anything like the world does now. It was little more than a watery ball of nothingness floating in the darkness.

Here's the bit that you'll need your brain for. To brighten things up God decided that the next thing He was going to create was light. What a good idea. Some pretty stars to illuminate the night sky and a sun to give daylight. Nope. As barmy as it sounds God created light without any of that. The Bible says that God gave the command for light to appear and it did.

Interested to know when the stars and the sun were created?

YEP, I'VE HAD ENOUGH OF BEING BAMBOOZLED!

Go to Bible book Genesis, chapter 1 and verses 14 to 17.

# BOY BANNED

The poor Israelites had been stuck in Egypt for hundreds of years having been reduced to being lowly slaves of the Pharaoh (Egypt's ruler). What a long way they'd come since the day their ancestor Joseph had been the Pharaoh's right hand man and they'd enjoyed the very best of living in Egypt. Their downfall had come with a change of Pharaoh. This one didn't care a jot that Joseph had helped saved their nation from ruin when it was struck by a famine. As far as he was concerned the Israelites were outsiders and didn't deserve to be treated the same as the Egyptians. In fact why hadn't anybody thought of it before? Thousands upon thousands of immigrant Israelites were the very workforce Egypt needed to help build their cities. Not only that but if they were made slaves he wouldn't have to pay them a thing. So that's what happened. The Israelites ended up serving the Egyptians as slaves.

What horrid Pharaoh hadn't bargained for was that because the Israelites were God's special nation, God still had plans for them to prosper despite their circumstances. So even though they were slaves the Israelite population kept on growing and growing. There was absolutely no stopping them and Egypt's Pharaoh was getting a bit edgy. The penny began to drop that if their numbers kept on growing at the same rate of knots, before

long there'd very soon be more Israelites than Egyptians. Yikes!
That spelled danger. Something had to be done, and pronto,
before the Israelites rose up and overthrew them!

Pharaoh ordered his slave masters to crack the whip and
make the Israelites work harder. If he could just grind them
into the ground there would be no chance of a rebellion. But
the population grew even more! Egypt's ruler was running
scared so he summoned the midwives who served the Israelites
and told them to kill all the baby boys as they were being born.
These brave ladies were going to do no such thing and made
out that the babies were born before they could get there.

Pharaoh was getting
desperate and ended up doing
a tragically barmy thing.

Read what it was in
Bible book Exodus,
chapter 1 and verse 22.

# 26

# STAFF CHANGES

This Bible story is all about who should lead the Israelite nation. God's No. 1 choice was a chap called Moses. Okay so Moses hadn't wanted the job when God first offered it to him but he eventually came round and ended up leading God's special nation out of slavery in Egypt.

With life in Egypt behind them the Israelites were on their way to the land of Canaan which God had given them as a place to live. You'd have thought they'd be over the moon to be free at last but, in no time at all, they were mumbling and grumbling about how horrible things were without a roof over their heads and not knowing where their next meal was coming from. The fact that God was looking after them didn't seem to count for anything.

When they did finally reach Canaan they decided not to go in because they were scared of its inhabitants. Just when you thought that the Israelites couldn't do anything else to try God's patience there was a revolt. A guy called Korah along with a few hundred other revolting Israelites (a little joke of mine) went head to head with Moses and his brother Aaron. Why should the pair of them be in charge? Er, because God had chosen them to do the job, that's why! God wasn't going to put up with rebellion in the camp and the Bible says that the ground

cracked open and swallowed Korah and his whole family alive!

The rest of the rebels were burned to a cinder by fire from heaven.

Now you'd think that they'd have learned their lesson, but no. Barmy as it may seem Moses and Aaron got the blame for these gory deaths so God sent a deathly plague to teach the disgruntled Israelites one more lesson.

Right, it was time to put an end to this once and for all. Moses got the leader of each of Israel's tribes to write their names on a wooden staff. Aaron was one of them. Moses then took them to the tabernacle tent where they worshipped God. Here was the deal. God was going to make one of the staffs sprout. Whoever that staff belonged to was God's choice and that would be the end of all that grumbling.

Discover who God picked in Bible book Numbers, chapter 17 and verses 8 to 12.

King Saul (of Israel) had taken a young lad called David under his wing. The reason for this was that David had given Saul's army victory over their Philistine enemies. It had begun with David defeating the Philistine warrior, Goliath – a big relief to Saul. David then went on to lead the Israelites to victory after victory, so much so that the grateful king promoted David to one of the army's top commanders. Things were looking up for David, the shepherd boy from Bethlehem.

But they started to go sour when Saul discovered that David's popularity was outshining his. David was the man of the moment and people even made up songs about him, saying how great he was and how he had killed more people in battle than King Saul. The king decided that this simply wouldn't do. A little bit of credit for David was okay but no way was this young upstart going to out-do him in the popularity stakes. He was Israel's main man and that was the way it was going to stay!

Something had to be done about David, and fast. It didn't help that Saul's son (Jonathan) had become best buddies with the king's young rival. Saul was eaten up with jealousy and wanted David dead and buried. Had he forgotten that God had lined up David to replace him as Israel's next king? To fight against David was to fight against God and that would be just barmy.

King Saul didn't seem to care a jot. The last thing on his warped mind was worrying about what God thought. All that mattered to him was getting rid of David.

One day, when David was in the royal palace, serenading seething Saul with a harp, the king's barminess came to a head. Want to check out the lengths the king would go to to finish David off?

Find out in Bible book 1 Samuel, chapter 19 and verses 9 to 10.

# 28

# PROPHET OF DOOM

During the course of its history the nation of Israel had a bit of a tiff and as a result it split into two. Boo hoo! The top bit kept the name Israel (which was quite handy for them) and the bottom bit took the name Judah. Israel very quickly gained a reputation for doing their own thing and ignoring God. Israel's first king after the bust up was a fella called Jeroboam. Instead of sacrificing to God in Jerusalem's Temple (like all good kings should) he burnt sacrifices to other gods on his own altar. God was totally unimpressed by this and sent a prophet from Judah to tell him so. As a sign that what he said was from God the altar was going to be split in two.

The king didn't like the prophet's message one little bit and commanded him to be seized. As Jeroboam stretched out his hand towards the guy, to his horror his arm shrivelled up. The king pleaded with the prophet to get God to make him better and sure enough He did. As a big thank you King Jeroboam invited the man of God round to his place for a slap up meal. Thanks but no thanks. God had told the prophet not to eat or drink anything while he was running this errand so he said his farewells and headed back to Judah.

As he made his way home he was met by another prophet. This old boy had heard from his sons about the recent goings on with Jeroboam and also invited the prophet back for a bite to eat. Once again the prophet from Judah declined but the old prophet wouldn't take no for an answer. Lying through his teeth he said that an angel had told him to do this. Well, you can't argue with an angel can you?

Who knows why the old prophet told such a whopper of a porky pie (lie) but no sooner had they finished the meal than God had a message for his misguided messenger. It's a barmy ending for sure!

IT'D BE NICE TO HAVE SOME GOOD NEWS JUST ONCE IN A WHILE!

Find out what it was in Bible book 1 Kings, chapter 13 and verses 20 to 26.

# 29

# HERE TODAY ...

There aren't that many characters from the Bible who have an expression named after them but here are a few. 'The patience of Job' (a guy who went through a bit of rough patch), 'As old as Methuselah' (he lived to a whopping 969 years old!) and 'The wisdom of Solomon' (Israel's third king). Solomon's dad (David) had reigned as Israel's king for forty years and he was a tough act to follow. Solomon knew first-hand what it took to please the people but more importantly he knew what it took to please God.

Soon after he became king, God appeared to Solomon in a dream and told him to ask whatever he wanted and it was his. Cor! There's an offer you can't refuse. Top of Solomon's list was wisdom.

God was as good as His word and gave the king the wisdom that he'd asked for. Not only that but God also made Solomon successful and rich in everything he did ...

It proved to be the best decision that Solomon ever made. His wisdom helped him build a temple for God, a palace for himself, make the nation rich beyond anyone's wildest dreams and solve difficult dilemmas.

Sad to say Solomon's glory days didn't last. He became so rich and powerful that anything was his for the taking. This

included wives, of which he had 700, and concubines (wives of less importance) of which he had 300. That makes a grand total of 1,000! The Bible says that it was his wives who were eventually his downfall. Why's that? Solomon made the barmy mistake of paying more attention to the gods of some of his wives than to the God who had made him king in the first place. God wasn't pleased one little bit and told Solomon so. From then on things went from bad to worse. It seemed to Solomon that the good times were gone for good and all because he'd disobeyed God.

Want to get a flavour of what was going through the downcast king's head?

Check out Bible book Ecclesiastes, chapter 1 and verses 1 and 2.

# 30

# TAX TRICK

There are some people you can pick a fight with and it's a walkover. (I'm not talking about a fisticuffs fight here but a war of words.) The Jewish religious leaders were a bunch of guys who were forever trying to trip Jesus up and get one over on Him. But when it came to picking a fight with Jesus you'd have thought that they would have learned their lesson. For sure, it was pretty obvious that they considered Jesus to be a threat to them and they certainly didn't like what He did or the way that He did it. To make matters worse the crowds adored Jesus and couldn't get enough of Him. But, rather than taking a leaf out of their book and actually listening to what Jesus had to say (and learning from it) the religious leaders were continually looking for ways to pull Jesus down. How barmy is that? Because Jesus was God's Son, and because He was filled with God's Holy Spirit, He got the better of them time after time. Jesus didn't need to use a lot of smart one-liners to upstage these guys. He had God's wisdom to cut through all of their treachery and trickery.

That's how Jesus got one over on the devil when he tried to lure Him away from what God had sent Jesus to earth to do. The devil came at Jesus with words from the Bible to trip Him

up but he used them in a way that God had never intended. With God's wisdom inside Him Jesus put the devil straight and sent His enemy packing.

The religious leaders used the same sort of tactics to entice Jesus to make a wrong move. They dispatched a bunch of their guys to ask Jesus a question. After buttering up Jesus with a spot of sweet-talking they cut to the chase. They wanted to know, in Jesus' opinion, who they should pay taxes to. Was it to God or was it to Caesar (the Roman ruler of their nation)?

If Jesus said God they'd accuse Him of rebelling against Caesar and make sure the Romans knew about it.

If Jesus said Caesar they'd accuse Him of rebelling against God and make sure the adoring crowds knew about it.

Either way their cunning plan was to discredit Jesus. Did they succeed?

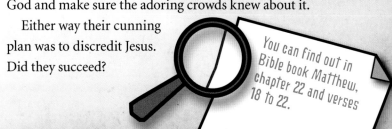

You can find out in Bible book Matthew, chapter 22 and verses 18 to 22.

# 31

# TOPSY TURVY TEAM

I f you were God (which you're not) then the chances are there are some things that you'd do differently. For instance would you send your only Son (Jesus) down to earth, to be born as a baby and to take the punishment for all the things we've done wrong? Not sure? Well, God did.

Or would you create human beings (like God did), make a wonderful world for them to live in (like God did also) and then leave these human beings in charge of your creation? Not sure again? Well, God did this too.

If you mulled it over long enough I'm sure that one of the things you'd do differently would be something to do with who Jesus picked to be His disciples. (These were the band of twelve guys who went everywhere with Jesus while He was on the earth.) Jesus wasn't stupid. He knew all along that once He'd gone back to heaven (with His mission accomplished), this motley bunch of guys were going to be left running the show. So, when I tell you that some of them were uneducated fishermen, one of them was a tax collector who probably diddled people out of their money and the rest were just a bunch of ordinary guys, you'd start to get a bit worried that it would all go wrong once Jesus was off the scene, wouldn't you?

Even while Jesus was with these fellas they sometimes

made a mess of things. One of them (Peter) made out he didn't have anything to do with Jesus to protect his own skin. A couple of them (James and John) were more concerned about getting a front row seat in heaven than anything else. And one of them (Thomas) took a lot of convincing that Jesus had been raised from the dead.

But what seems absolutely barmy to you and me makes complete sense to God. God isn't looking for people who've got it sussed. He's looking for people who will rely on His life and power. Not convinced that Jesus can make a difference to a person's life?

# 32

# SOW THERE!

Jesus loved to tell stories to explain things about God. Once He told a story about a farmer who went out to sow some seed. In those days they didn't have machines to do the job; it was all done by hand. As the farmer strode up and down his field he flung the seed to the right and to the left. Some of it fell on the good soil where the farmer intended but some of the seed landed on the path, some among the rocks and stones and some, unfortunately, in the thorns.

The seed that fell on the path didn't stay there long. As far as some hungry birds were concerned it was dinner-time and they gobbled the seed up. Slurp! The seed that fell on the rocky ground didn't fare much better. Okay, so there was a dusting of soil on the ground and the seed began to grow, but not for long. When the sun came up the seedlings were scorched under the heat of the day and shrivelled because they had next to no root. The seed sown among the thorns shot up but was then choked to death by its thorny neighbours. Last up was the seed that fell on the good soil. No prizes for guessing that this produced a bumper harvest for the farmer.

If a farmer knew all of this you'd think he'd be barmy not to take a bit more care with how he planted his seed, wouldn't you? Good point and this was what Jesus was trying to get

across – except that He wasn't talking about seed that is sown in fields but seed that God wants to sow in our hearts. The Bible says that God's words (in the Bible) are like seeds and when we allow them to take root they can change our lives for the better. It's like having a mahoosive harvest of good things from God in our hearts.

Jesus explained that we need to be careful that God's enemy (the devil) doesn't snatch His Word from our hearts, like the birds. We need to be careful that we don't allow the ups and downs of life to let God's Word in our hearts wither and die like the seed in the rocky places. And we need to be careful that we don't get so caught up in the busyness of life that God's Word in our hearts is choked to death, like the thorns choked the seeds.

Want to know the best choice to make? Head for Bible book Matthew, chapter 13 and verse 23.

# 33

# FUNNY FOE

Don't you just love springtime? Daffodils and crocuses popping up all over the place, cute bunnies bouncing in the meadows and not forgetting blood, guts and gore spilling out on the battlefield? Lovely isn't it? This barmy Bible story tells us that springtime was the time when kings went off to war. What a nice way to make the most of the lighter evenings! The Israelites were no exception and King David sent his troops off to do battle with the Ammonites and to besiege the city of Rabbah. Having razed it to the ground David became the proud owner of the enemy king's rather impressive crown. (It weighed about seventy-five pounds and was made of solid gold.)

The Israelites' next battle was with their arch enemy (and near neighbour), the pesky Philistines. With God's help the Israelites were victorious in one battle after another. If you know anything about the Philistines then you've probably heard about Goliath. He was a gargantuan guy (a giant in fact) who stood at over nine feet tall! David had killed Goliath before becoming king but the fearsome fella also had a brother called Lahmi. Although the Bible doesn't say that he was a giant, it does tell us that his spear had a shaft like a weaver's rod just like Goliath so there's a good chance he was a big 'un as well.

Anyway, in one of these skirmishes Lahmi was also killed.

If you're wondering when we're going to get to the barmy bit your wait is over. In yet another battle that the Israelites fought at a place called Gath, they came face-to-face with a rather unusual foe. He made the mistake of taunting the Israelites to the point that King David's narked nephew (Jonathan) had had enough and finished the guy off. But to discover the barmy bit you're going to need to go on the warpath yourself.

AW, SHUCKS! I LOVE SPRING!

Head for Bible book 1 Chronicles, chapter 20 and verse 6 and 7.

# 34

# REST DAY RUMPUS

**A**s far as many of Israel's religious leaders were concerned Jesus was a bit of a rebel. They spent most of their time trying to obey God's laws and also to abide by all of their man-made rules and regulations and they expected everyone else to do the same. Jesus thought that they'd lost the plot. God's laws were put in place to make life better and help people understand what God is like. They weren't there to make life an absolute misery which is what the religious leaders seemed to do.

Saturday was when the Jewish people took time out to worship God and to rest from the work of the week. When God had created the world He did it in six days and put His feet up on day seven. But the Sabbath certainly wasn't meant to be a day on which you could do next to nothing, for fear of getting in trouble with God (which was what the religious leaders had made it). Jesus was about to naff off these guys not once but twice on the Sabbath day and they weren't going to like it one little bit.

The first incident happened when Jesus and His disciples (His trusty band of twelve men), walking through a corn field, started picking off the ears of the corn to munch as a tasty snack. The religious leaders accused the disciples of breaking the Sabbath but Jesus would have none of it. As far

as He was concerned the Sabbath day was there for people to enjoy, not to make life harder.

The second head-to-head was in a synagogue (that's sort of like a Jewish church) where Jesus was confronted by a chap whose hand was completely withered. The religious leaders were lurking, waiting for Jesus to step over the line and do something of which they could accuse Him. They weren't the least bit bothered about the mangled man. Their only concern was to make it clear to Jesus that healing someone on the Sabbath was a big no-no. That didn't wash with Jesus one bit.

To find out what Jesus had to say look up Bible book Matthew, chapter 12 and read verses 11 through to 14.

Abram was in a bit of a quandary. God had hand-picked him to kick-start a brand-new nation that would love God and through whom God would show the world how much He loved them.

So far, so good. Abram (who was later known as Abraham) had uprooted himself and his family and travelled to the land of Canaan where God had told him this nation would be based. That sounded good as well. And God also told Abram that his descendants would be as numerous as the stars in the sky. Awesome! Er, not quite. Just one teensy problem. Abram and his wife Sarai (who was later known as Sarah) didn't have any kids and kids were one thing that you most definitely needed to have descendants. Just to make matters worse, Abram and Sarai were getting on a bit and, to be perfectly honest, their chances of having a family were extremely slim. Put all that into the melting pot and it looked like God's great plans for this new nation were going to be scuppered before they'd even got off the starting blocks.

Fear not! God wasn't getting stressed about it. No sir'ee! God paid Abram a visit to say that not only would He look after him and the bit about his descendants being like the stars in the sky, but He'd also give him great prosperity. But

Abram had a bone to pick with God. What was the point of God making him wealthy if he had nobody to pass it on to? The way things stood at that moment his servant Eliezer was lined up to get the lot.

It seemed like Abram needed reminding that God was on his case and that when God says He's going to do something, He will.

What happened next probably seemed a bit barmy to Abram. God instructed him to go fetch a heifer, a goat, a ram, a dove and a young pigeon which he chopped in two (except for the birds). Abram laid the halves opposite each other on the ground and then God sent him into a deep sleep. For your info, God was making a covenant (sort of like a contract) with Abram.

# 36

# MIRACLE MAN

**W**hen it comes to God don't ever make the mistake of thinking that anything is impossible for Him. Actually the Bible tells us, loud and clear, that God is bigger and better than any of us so what seems like a complete non-starter to you or me is easy peasy for Him. I mean, who else could create the universe out of nothing whatsoever and then make the world's first woman (Eve) out of the rib of the world's first man (Adam)? Well, God could and, more to the point, that's precisely what He did do.

So, when God wanted to patch up the friendship between us and Him, He had a plan up His sleeve. Because a man had rebelled against God (that was Adam) and broken our relationship with Him, it needed a man to get us back together with God again.

This man was going to have to take the punishment for all the wrong stuff that we do but there was just one problem. This man had to be perfect, through and through, which ruled out every single man who has ever lived. The Bible says that absolutely everyone is on the wrong side of God and there's nothing any of us can do to change that.

Where on earth, then, was God going to find a mint-condition man? Well, not from earth, that's for sure. So how about from

heaven? Now you're talking. As I said, nothing's impossible when it comes to God. Here's what God came up with. His idea was to send His one and only Son (Jesus) down to earth to take the punishment on our behalf. Wow, how amazing was that!

But Jesus couldn't just pop down from heaven. For a start it would probably scare the pants off us if we saw Him in all His glory; He needed to show up as a man. Hmm, that sounds tricky. Not for God though. If you know anything about the Christmas story then you'll know about an angel paying a visit to a gal called Mary in the town of Nazareth. Mary was going to be Jesus' mum and God was going to make her pregnant with God's Son. That's how God was going to get the job done.

Want to know all the ins and outs of this barmy sounding (but totally true) story?

Then take a look in Bible book Luke, chapter 1 and verse 35.

# 37

# A MOVING STORY

**H**ave you ever moved house? If you have then you'll know that there's a lot of hard work involved before you can 'up sticks' and settle down in your new home. Most people hire a removal firm to cart all their worldly possessions from one house to the other. It's a big job because there's usually heaps and heaps of stuff to be transported in the removal van.

Jesus told a parable (a made-up story with a meaning) about a chap who was on the move but, sad to say, his final destination wasn't what he was hoping for. Here's how it happened.

Jesus had been asked by someone what it was that they needed to do to get to heaven when they died. That was a good question to ask and Jesus decided to answer it with a timely tale about a rich man.

Jesus began by explaining that the man in the story had done pretty well for himself in life, and nothing wrong with that! He was obviously a farmer because Jesus said that he'd just had a bumper harvest but wasn't quite sure where he was going to store his abundance of crops. After a bit of 'umming' and 'ahhing' he decided to pull down the barns that he already had and set about building some even bigger ones. The man began to be a bit smug about his good fortune and the success very quickly went to his head. He thought that being rich was the best thing ever and he planned to enjoy every single minute of it. The greedy guy stashed away his wealth and produce in his big new barns and gave himself a pat on the back for hitting the big time. Now he could put his feet up, enjoy his wealth and simply look after No. 1 (which meant himself).

The man's barmy mistake is that he'd not given a thought to what would happen when he died. You can't get a removal firm to take your riches with you when your time is up on earth. So what did Jesus have to say on the matter?

WHY ALL THE FUSS? I LOVE MOVING HOME.

Find out in Bible book Luke, chapter 12 and verses 20 and 21.

## 38
# SOME BODY SPECIAL

The death of Jesus had been a big blow for His disciples and His other followers. After three years of hanging around God's one and only Son, as He revealed to people what God is like, it was a shock to see their Master crucified and die. Three days later all that changed and to their utter amazement Jesus came back from the dead. Jesus had taken the punishment for the things we do wrong which is why He was executed (the Bible says He died by crucifixion) and now God's power had brought Jesus back to life. But there was something different about the resurrected Jesus. On the one hand His disciples sort of knew it was Him because of the way He spoke to them and because He still bore the scars on His body from His crucifixion. Then again Jesus' body now allowed Him to do things that were impossible for normal human beings. For one thing Jesus could appear and disappear at the drop of the hat. One minute He'd be there and the next He wouldn't. And Jesus could walk through walls without injuring Himself (which He did once when He wanted to meet up with His disciples in an upstairs room).

It was as if Jesus had a body like that of the angels. He could use it in heaven but He could also use it on earth.

Either way, it was like nothing anybody had ever seen before, and everyone was amazed.

Over a period of forty days Jesus showed up time and again to His followers to prove that He was alive and well. A couple of them had met Jesus while they were travelling to a place called Emmaus. As they recounted this to their friends, Jesus appeared again. Da-Dah! Between you and me they were a little taken aback and thought that Jesus was a ghost.

Jesus soon put their minds at rest and quelled their quivering. He told them to go ahead and touch His body, then they would see that He wasn't a spooky spectre; He was flesh and bones just like they were.

As if to emphasise this point Jesus then did something that probably could have seemed barmy.

Read it in Bible book Luke, chapter 24 and verses 41 to 43.

# 39

# DOUBLE-TALKING DISCIPLE

This barmy Bible story features a guy called Peter who was one of Jesus' twelve disciples. Peter was sometimes a bit of a hot-head but Jesus thought he was great. God makes us all with different personalities and doesn't want us all to be the same. Peter certainly wasn't the sort of guy you'd expect the Son of God (Jesus) to have on His team. Peter wasn't afraid of mouthing off or using his sword if he had to. But God always looks at people's hearts and Peter's was sold out for Jesus so that was what mattered above everything else. Everywhere Jesus went Peter followed, hanging on His Master's every word and seeing first-hand the awesome healings and miracles that Jesus did.

Nobody had ever seen the like of Jesus before but who actually was He? Was Jesus just a good man who went about doing good things? Was He perhaps a prophet of God like one of the prophets from the olden days? Or was He something else? Jesus knew full well that people were asking these sorts of questions about Him and one particular time He asked His disciples, straight up, what the word on the street was about Him. Who did people say that He was? The disciples told Jesus that some people figured He was John the Baptist and others, maybe one of the great prophets like Elijah or Jeremiah.

Then Jesus posed the same question to Peter. What was his take on things? Who did Peter think He was? Peter had no doubt about it. Jesus was the Messiah (a special person sent by God) who would rescue the world *and* He was God's Son. Full marks to Peter. He was spot on. Jesus told him that he'd downloaded that piece of info directly from God in heaven. Now here's the barmy bit. While Peter had got it right about Jesus being our rescuer, he didn't like it when Jesus then told His disciples that He was going to be arrested and executed in Jerusalem to make all this possible. No way! Peter wasn't having that and he told Jesus so. To be fair to Peter he was only trying to protect his Master and Jesus knew Satan was using Peter to try and prevent Him from accomplishing His mission on earth. What did Jesus say to Peter?

# 40

# BIG BARNY

on't you just love double-acts like Batman and Robin, Ben and Jerry (of ice cream fame) and Paul and Barnabas (the stars of this Bible story)? You might already know a thing or two about Paul. He pops up all over the place in the New Testament bit of the Bible and, more to the point, he wrote a whopping great chunk of it! Barnabas is a less-known chap but he does get a few mentions. One of these was for selling a field (that he owned, otherwise that would have been stealing, wouldn't it?) and giving the proceeds to the church to help poor people. On top of that we are also told that his name means 'son of encouragement'. Isn't that nice?

Paul (who was originally called Saul) and Barnabas had worked together for a year in a place called Antioch. By way of an aside, this was where followers of Jesus were first given the nickname 'Christians'. Barnabas had been sent out by the church in Jerusalem to lend the Christians in Antioch a hand as the church there went from strength to strength. Now Barnabas roped in Paul to come and join him.

But the church in Antioch didn't want to keep this dynamic duo to themselves and sent the pair off with their blessing to do their stuff elsewhere. In one of the places they visited (Lystra), Paul and Barnabas got treated like

gods because Paul healed a crippled man. Things turned
sour when they shunned the limelight and gave the credit
to God. The two of them shared the good times and they
shared the bad times. They seemed inseparable which is
why what happened next sounds a bit barmy. When you've
gone through thick and thin with someone it seems daft to
let a petty squabble come between you but that's just what
happened to Paul and Barnabas.

Paul had an idea. How about they go back to the places they'd
visited on their travels and check up on the Christians while
they were there? Yep, Barnabas was
up for it and had a good idea
of his own. How about taking
John Mark with them too?

To read about Paul
and Barnabas' bust-
up go to Bible book
Acts, chapter 15 and
verses 37 to 40.

# 41

# ON SECOND THOUGHTS...

The Israelites had a lot to be grateful for as far as having a leader like Moses was concerned. In this Bible story we find out why. Here's the low-down on what was occurring.

The Israelites were waiting for Moses to come down from Mount Sinai after a forty-day meet up with God. To be honest they were getting a little impatient with the waiting. It seemed to them like he'd been gone forever and they were getting bored hanging around at the foot of the mountain twiddling their thumbs. As time wore on they sidled up to Moses' big brother, Aaron, to find out what was going on. By the sounds of it Aaron was ticked off kicking his heels as well and decided to take the matter into his own hands. He had a quick whip round the Israelites for any gold jewellery, melted it down and fashioned a rather natty golden calf.

What a creative fellow he was. This wasn't just a pretty bit of sculpture though. The gold idol had been made so that they could worship it (instead of the God who had been looking after them all the while). But they didn't bet on what God might think or how He'd feel. Because God is God He knows everything and can see everything. That included the shenanigans that the Israelites were getting up to with their golden calf.

God was livid with what the Israelites had done and let

Moses know in no uncertain words. God told Moses to leave Him alone while He dealt with those stiff-necked Israelites. He was planning to wipe out the lot of them but Moses wasn't quite so keen on the idea and said so to God.

Moses hastily reminded God of the promises that He'd made to Abraham, Isaac and Jacob (the founding fathers of Israel) about how He'd make them as numerous as the stars in the sky. If the Israelites were obliterated that wasn't going to be possible. And for that matter, what would all the other nations say? They'd think that God had planned this all along and that He wasn't the good God that Moses knew Him to be. Was Moses barmy to think he could persuade God to change His mind?

# 42
# HOLY HIPPY

In the Old Testament part of the Bible there's lots of stuff about sacrificing various things to God and loads of rules and regulations you had to follow to keep in God's good books. None of it was designed to make life difficult. It was all there to help people understand what God is like and how different He is from you and me. When God created human beings they didn't have to bother with any of this sort of stuff because they were perfect in God's eyes. But, as soon as people began to turn their backs on God, the rot set in. God hadn't changed one little bit, but people had.

When God had made the world's first two people (Adam and Eve) it was easy to see the reflection of God's life in them. Over time it become harder and harder to see what God was like by looking at mankind. So God showed the Israelite nation different things they could do to remind themselves (and others) what He was really like.

One of the things that the Bible tells us about God is that He is holy. That doesn't mean He's got lots of holes in Him! It means God's completely different from us. He's pure. He's good. And He's got absolutely no interest whatsoever in doing bad stuff. That's good to know isn't it?

While a chap called Moses was leading the Israelites, God

told him that if a guy or a gal wanted to take time out to live in a super-duper holy sort of way for a bit then here's how they could do it. For starters they'd need to sign on the dotted line by making a vow (a promise) to God to separate themselves from the rest of the people. Part of the deal was that not a single drop of alcohol could pass their lips until their time was up. Next up they wouldn't be allowed to let a razor go anywhere near their hair. It was the long-haired hippy look for them. There were other things that God instructed these people to do as well which might sound barmy but God knew that it would help them to rediscover what God is like.

Bible book Numbers, chapter 6 and verses 1 and 2 will tell you what these people were called.

# CLOUD NAV

**A**lthough this book is called *50 Barmiest Bible Stories* you've probably worked out by now that there's nothing barmy about God Himself or the Bible. The only thing that's barmy in all of this is that the things people do, or some of the things God does, look barmy to some people. But they always make a lot of sense to God! For instance it might seem a tad barmy God coming down from heaven to live in a tent. What, you didn't know that God was into camping? Well, let me assure you He was, and big style.

There was a time when the Israelites didn't have a land to call home and were wandering from place to place, pitching up camp whenever God told them to. But it wasn't only the Israelites who lived in tents. God did too. It was God who had started their nation in the first place so He was keen to make sure that He remained at the centre of everything they did. That meant living among them. How did God do that? By having His very own tent. Let's be clear about this, when I say tent I don't mean a bog-standard tent just large enough for an average Israelite family to squeeze into. Nope! The tent we're talking about here was called the tabernacle and it was as big as a large marquee and set inside a high perimeter fence. The tabernacle was God's idea and He'd designed it down to its very last tent peg. Everything about God's tent was tip-top and laden with gold, silver and bronze.

Now you're probably wondering how on earth God fitted into the tabernacle tent, however large it was. One thing you do need to know is that God didn't leave heaven while all this was going on (just in case you were thinking that everything would fall apart while He was down here). Because God is God it means that He can be in more than one place at the same time. This is very convenient for God but not so easy for me to explain. What the Israelites did see of God was a cloud of His presence that covered the tabernacle by day and looked like fire at night.

Want to find out some interesting info about this cloud?

Take a trip to Bible book Numbers, chapter 9 and verses 17 to 23.

# RUMBLE GRUMBLE

You'd have thought that the Israelites would have been well-pleased to have left Egypt where they'd been held as slaves for hundreds of years. Not a bit of it! No sooner had they escaped from their Egyptian slave masters (thanks to God parting the waters of the Red Sea and then drowning the Egyptian army who were chasing them), than they'd begun to mumble and moan about how tough life was on the road. In no time at all they were beginning to see their days in Egypt through rose-tinted glasses. Their barmy thinking went something like this. Okay, so they'd had to work their fingers to the bone from dawn to dusk to make bricks for Egypt's cities but at least they'd had a roof over their heads and a bit more choice when it came to their menu.

The fact that God was miraculously providing them with manna (which tasted like wafers made with honey) in the morning and a fresh supply of quail (birds) every evening didn't seem to count for a thing. And, while they were at it, the Israelites also had a thing or two to say about the lack of water in the desert – as if God hadn't thought of that as well before He'd brought them there. When they needed spring water God led them to it. When there were no springs to be found God produced gushing water from a rock. But still

they grumbled. Was there no pleasing them? Moses their leader was cheesed off having his ears bent all the time about how hard things were. Not a word of thanks about how God had rescued them or that they were headed for a land of their own to settle in. Ungrateful wotsits!

And it wasn't only Moses who was fed up with their continual sniping. God was as well. In this barmy Bible story God eavesdrops on a bunch of moaners and groaners and decides that enough is enough.

Read about it in Bible book Numbers, chapter 11 and verses 1 to 3.

# KING-SIZED KIP

The great thing about the Bible is that not only does it tell you all about God and how we can get to know Him but it also has loads of interesting, random bits of information in it as an added bonus.

There's a barmy bit like that at the end of this Bible story but I'm going to leave it to you to look it up. Meanwhile, we catch up with the Israelites as they are travelling through the open countryside on their way to the land of Canaan. It had been forty long years since they'd begun their journey and they would have arrived a whole lot earlier if most of their fighting men hadn't been scaredy cats and chosen not to enter Canaan for fear of its inhabitants. Now, with all of those lily-livered wimps dead and buried, God was giving His special nation a second chance.

As the Israelites drew nearer and nearer to their destination the tension was mounting. They had to pass through the lands of other kings and an enemy ambush was a very real possibility. God had warned them that when they passed through the lands of Seir and Moab they were not to look for a fight. These people were under God's hand of protection and were to be treated with respect because their ancestors had honoured Him. Once they'd passed through, the Israelites were free to go to war and to conquer the land.

First on the list was Heshbon which was ruled by King Sihon the Amorite. The Israelites beat the Heshbonites to a pulp (with God's help) without any bother and on they moved to their next conquest. It was Og, king of Bashan, who they now had in their sights. King Og's territory amounted to sixty cities and the Bible tells us that the Israelites took them one after another, destroying the lot of 'em. The fact that the cities were fortified with high walls didn't seem to slow their progress a jot. And now for that barmy fact that I promised you at the beginning …

# 46
# PA-IN-LAW'S PLAN

Moses was leading the Israelites to the land of Canaan but on the way he decided to make a bit of a detour to pay a visit to Jethro, his father-in-law. Jethro lived in the land of Midian and that's where Moses had ended up after he'd done a runner from Egypt (having killed an Egyptian). Just when his whole world seemed to be going pear-shaped Moses met Zipporah (one of Jethro's daughters) and they got married and lived happily ever after in Midian. Well no, nice as it sounds, that's not quite how the story ended actually. The happy couple did settle down in Midian and have a couple of kids (Gershom and Eliezer) but at the ripe old age of eighty, (having spent forty years in Midian), God sent Moses back to Egypt to rescue the Israelites from slavery. Zipporah and the boys joined Moses for the jaunt but on their return Moses sent them on ahead of him back to his father-in-law. Who knows why? Maybe Moses didn't want his family to have to trudge endlessly through the wilderness, which is what happened to the rest of the Israelites because of their disobedience to God.

Anyway, as I mentioned, Moses popped in to say 'hi' to Jethro (and also to his wife and kids). Jethro got to hear first-hand about all of the amazing miracles that God had performed to free the Israelites.

The next day Moses was up bright and early. There was work to be done. As Israel's leader his job was to sit as judge over all of the people's disputes. When you realise that there could have been well over two million of them in total it's no surprise that Moses was up to his ears in disagreements which he was expected to settle. The Bible says that the irked Israelites stood round him from dawn to dusk waiting to hear his verdict. Jethro had something to say on the matter and he told Moses straight. It was utterly barmy doing it single-handed. Moses would be run ragged in no time if he carried on like that. Want to hear about Jethro's helpful suggestion?

You can find it in Bible book Exodus, chapter 18 and verses 19 to 23.

# 47
# PESKY PLAGUES

Egypt's Pharaoh was a tough nut to crack. He'd set himself up against God and no way was he going to allow the Israelites (God's special nation) to be released from being Egypt's slaves. A guy called Moses had the job of trying to persuade the immovable monarch to change his mind, but that didn't look like it was going to happen any time soon.

Pharaoh held on to the Israelites with an iron grip but, little by little, God's plan was to prise his fingers off His prize people. Turning all the water in the land to blood and infesting it with frogs hadn't worked so God lined up some more pesky plagues to see if Pharaoh would change his mind. God told Moses to strike the dry ground with his wooden staff and the dust became a plague of nasty gnats. Ugh! The place was swarming with the horrid insects. Did Pharaoh budge? No he didn't! Right, try this for size then, Pharaoh. How about a plague of flies? They swarmed everywhere in such numbers that the land was ruined. But Pharaoh wasn't playing ball. Throw your worst at him, he wasn't going to change his mind. Let's see about that. It was time to crank things up a bit. God sent a plague so terrible that it destroyed all of Egypt's livestock. Horses, donkeys, camels, cattle, sheep and goats; they were all wiped out. But not those of the Israelites. God protected them.

The barmy thing about this Bible story is how stiff-necked Pharaoh was. Imagine pitting yourself against God. It's a complete non-starter and a waste of time. You're never going to outsmart God. And guess what? That's how the story ends. God wins and Pharaoh loses – but how barmy of Egypt's ruler not to back down while the going was good.

There were still a few more plagues to go before all that happened and I'll let you read about one of the more painful ones for yourself.

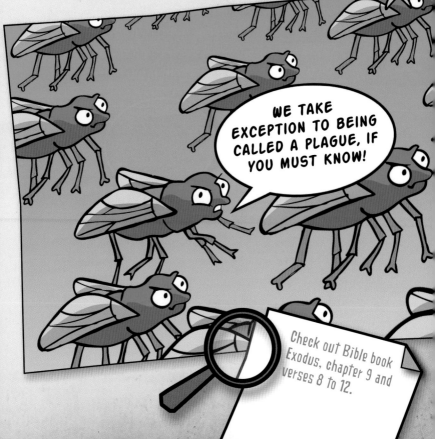

# 48
# SAUL'S FALL

Israel's very first king was a chap called Saul. Having a king wasn't God's idea. It was the Israelites who wanted a king to rule over them so that they could be just like all the other nations around them. For God's part, He'd wanted Israel to be different from everyone else so that He could be the One to look after His special people. Having warned the Israelites that having a king wasn't the best of ideas He let them have their way. King Saul looked every bit the regal ruler on the outside but actually he wasn't so good on the inside. To be fair to the guy he tried his best but, when push came to shove, Saul was more concerned about what other people thought about him than what God thought. And that was the beginning of his downfall.

Having been told by God to take his army to war against the Amalekites, King Saul mustered over 200,000 fighting men and went off to battle. God wanted the Amalekites taught a lesson that they'd never forget. Their ancestors had ambushed the Israelites centuries earlier (completely unprovoked) and now it was time for their come-uppance. God's orders to Saul were to wipe them out entirely. Even the sheep and cattle were to be destroyed. Nothing or no one was to remain alive. Couldn't be clearer. So off King Saul went with his army and attacked the Amalekites.

Just when it looked like everything was going to plan the prophet Samuel received an urgent message from God. Of all the barmy things, Saul had not only spared the life of the Amalekite king (Agag) but had also allowed his soldiers to hold on to some of the sheep and cattle for themselves.

Samuel headed for Saul with a face like thunder. Okay Saul, so what is this bleating of sheep and lowing of cattle that the prophet could hear? Could it be plunder of the sort that God had strictly forbidden? The king blurted out all manner of excuses for disobeying God but none of it was going to wash with seething Samuel. Eventually King Saul came clean and said that he'd been afraid of his soldiers and had given in to them (rather than obeying God).

Having told Saul that his days as king were numbered Samuel had one last piece of unfinished business to do.

Find out what it was in Bible book 1 Samuel, chapter 15 and verses 32 to 35.

# 49

# WIDOW CRANKY

There are loads of prophets mentioned in the Bible and one of the more well-known ones was a chap called Elijah.

Being a prophet of God wasn't always the easiest of jobs to do, particularly when it involved passing on messages from God that were less than complimentary. Why would that be? Well, not only did Israel (the land that Elijah lived in) have some jolly good kings, it unfortunately also had its fair share of bad 'uns.

One such bad king was a guy called Ahab. King Ahab didn't have much time for the God of Israel and preferred to worship the gods of his equally obnoxious wife, Jezebel. The background story to this barmy Bible bit is that Elijah had been on the run from Ahab after the prophet had commanded a drought to afflict Israel (as a punishment for the king's wicked ways).

Fret not, God saw to it that Elijah was fed and watered during those lean years, first by ravens (yes, you heard me right) and then by a widow whose supply of oil and flour miraculously didn't run out the whole time that Elijah lodged with her and her son.

Sometime later the son fell ill and took a turn for the worse until he finally breathed his last and died. I'm not sure what

Elijah made of it all but the weeping widow laid the blame for her son's death squarely at the perplexed prophet's feet. It was almost as if she was saying if Elijah hadn't showed up then none of this would ever have happened. A bit barmy, don't you think? After all it was thanks to Elijah that she and her son now had food in the house.

Elijah didn't take it personally. He went to her son, stretched himself out on the boy's dead body and prayed to God for the lad to come back to life.

THERE'S GRATITUDE FOR YOU!

To find out how the story ends go to 1 Kings, chapter 17 and verses 22 to 24.

# 50

# DISCO DAVID

It's completely barmy that some people have no problem enjoying a good old knees-up to celebrate a birthday or something like that but they get a wee bit uncomfortable when it comes to getting excited about God. Even more so, because it was God who first set an example. When God created the world it was He who made a point of saying that it was good, over and over again. God just loves us bigging things up and that's what this Bible story is about.

Israel's new king (David) had just got himself his very own royal city to live in (Jerusalem) and now he wanted to bring Israel's ark box there to stay. Just in case you didn't know, the ark was a golden box in which were kept two stone slabs. On them were engraved God's Ten Commandments to the Israelites. The ark was carried using long poles which were held by priests. The ark represented God being with them. This special box had travelled with the Israelites through much of their history and was very important to them.

Now that David was king, bringing the ark to Jerusalem was top of his list. He and his men set out to fetch it from a place called Baalah of Judah where it had been kept. It was loaded onto an ox cart and off they went. Everyone was having a high old time leaping and dancing and singing as the

procession wended its way back to Jerusalem. Then disaster
struck. One of the oxen lost its footing and a guy called Uzzah
reached out to stop the ark from falling. Zap! God struck
Uzzah down dead for not treating the ark with respect.

David decided to leave the ark at the house of Obed-Edom
while he figured out what to do next. For the three months it
was there Obed-Edom revelled in God's blessings. So, when
King David got wind of this, he decided to fetch the ark again.
But, this time he made sure the ark was carried properly by the
priests and not on any old cart. The king had learned his lesson.

Once again David and his entourage partied all the way
back to Jerusalem. The king even took off his royal robes to
celebrate. While God may have
loved it there was one person
who thought that the king
looked big-time barmy.

Find out who that
was in Bible book
2 Samuel, chapter 6
and verses 16 to 23.

# Get into God's Word.
## Every day.

**FOR AGES 7–11**

Join the Topz Gang as they explore the Bible through daily Bible readings, puzzles, cartoons and prayers!

**FOR AGES 11–14**

Read a bit of the Bible every day, explore lots of stuff about you and God – and crack puzzles along the way!

**Available as annual subscriptions or single issues, published every two months.**

# Learn about life with lots of laughs